Marriage Quotes

100 Lines, Sayings, Quotes for the Married

THE GRUMPY GURU

The Grumpy Guru

Printed in the United States of America

First Printing, 2018

ISBN: 9781983103995

http://thegrumpy.guru
http://365ways.me

This book is dedicated to all of you strong people who are taking responsibility of your own feelings and doing something to be better.

All my heartfelt gratitude to the following people: my mom Ruby Jane, you have made me everything I am today; my dad Nestor-- my eternal, my angel, and the source of my perseverance; Mommyling, my spiritual guide ; Ria & Joe, the true witnesses of my transformation and my foundation pillars; Ellie Jane, the sparkle of our eyes;

Juan, thanks for always encouraging me to push harder - you are my ONE; Rocco & Radha, my reason for everything.

The Love of my family and friends is the fountain of inspiration that never runs dry. Thank you for constantly inspiring me, motivating me, and loving me unconditionally.

This book will never be complete without the help of my trusted and talented friends, Roillan James Paña, and everyone at NOW for the moral support.

For reals, I am sick of Chicken Soup! It's not all rainbows and puppies in this world.

I put together a collection of various works to help me find inner strength and peace. I realized that sometimes we just need a real version of ways to feel better and go on with our daily lives.

I am The Grumpy Guru and I know grumpy more than the average grump. I realized that for whatever I am feeling, I had the power to switch to a more positive disposition with a little bit of guidance, a little bit of insight and a line or 2 of text.

I don't think I'll ever stop being grumpy but with the help of these snippets, I can channel them in a positive direction. If this works for me, I can only hope it will work for most people.

This is The Grumpy Guru's take to tackle and manage moments of darkness, doubt, and insecurity.

It's OK to be a grumpy, but Grumps can be Blissfully Happy, too.

I suggest you read what touches you, what helps you move on and what works for you. I've given you 365 different ways and it's up to you what you want to read in this book.

Trust me in my 41 years of grumpiness, I'm still here managing and coping and being relatively happy & content.

Cheers to you guys!

THE GRUMPY GURU

Let's All Be Blissfully Grumpy Together

Love is a splendid thing. We only understand it once we experienced it. Love knows no limits. It knows no ends. It is faithful and resists to sit and wait until it overflows to another being.

The Grumpy Guru

1

\\

Where you plant
love, life grows.

//

\\

It is when you are
fully seen for who
you are that you
know that you
are loved.

//

\\

To love means
to look on with
adoration despite
his or her
imperfections.

//

\\

Being in a
marriage is letting
go of prejudice
and pride.

//

\\

A good marriage
is letting go of
sleep because
living in reality
is better.

//

\\

Love recognizes
nothing except
hope.

//

\\

If you want to
build a successful
marriage, you
have to fall in love
with the same
person every day.

//

\\

Deeply loving someone gives you courage to face challenges in life.

//

\\

Being in a
marriage is being
compatible with
your weirdness.
Now that's
true love.

//

\\

Being joined
together in
marriage gives
each other
strength during
struggles, rest
in sorrow and
minister to
each other
when in need.

//

\\

Marriage is loving
more than love.

//

\\

We each have
a song that is
incomplete until
another comes
along to
complete it.

//

\\

You want to start the rest of your life now when you meet the right person to spend life with.

//

\\

Being in a marriage is taking in the worse and realizing the best of the person.

//

15

\\

Lasting love is like making a bread that had to be remade to create something new.

//

\\

Being in marriage is not taking from each other but helping each.

//

\\

Togetherness
means having
enough space
for heaven to
take place!

//

\\

No one who is
loved is ever poor.

//

\\

When you're in a marriage, you learn to enjoy the differences more than the similarities.

//

\\

A loving marriage is more than just being together. It's companionship.

//

\\

To grow in love is
to grow more love.

//

\\

A good marriage
is learning to love
each other in
a lifetime.

//

\\

Love at first sight is easy. A lasting relationship meant looking at the person as if it's always the first sight of love.

//

\\

A good question to ask when you're marrying: Can you imagine getting old with this person?

//

\\

A strong kind of
love carries you
through storms
in life alive.

//

\\

If you find the
same weirdness
with another,
you have found
true love!

//

\\

The right kind of love is what awakens passions and lets us reach for more.

//

\\

When you fall in love, it's hard to get back up again.

//

\\

Marriage is like taking the mundanity of everyday things and turn it into something golden.

//

\\

Finding the right partner is like getting the answer you have been searching for your entire life.

//

\\

Love sees beyond expectations and just love more.

//

\\

Love is a very important reason to get married.

//

\\

Marriage is a gift
that two people
can enjoy in
this lifetime.

//

\\

You can never fully find satisfaction from your partner. It must come from within and flows throughout.

//

\\

Deep commitment
is necessary
for a lasting
relationship.

//

\\

They say that love is work. Marriage is even harder!

//

\\

Once you know your true identity in God, you are a freely married person who can love more.

//

\\

A happy marriage consist of two people working together to make things work.

//

\\

Your spouse is not your source of happiness. If that was, how draining that would be!

//

\\

Instead of investing time to gratify the inward desires, your job is to look outward and love your partner.

//

\\

Sacrifice is what
true love looks like.

//

\\

True love waits.

//

\\

Being truly in love means being committed to love.

//

\\

Being
wholehearted to
marriage starts
by recognizing
the value of
the person.

//

\\

You will invest in
something that
you find valuable.
So does marriage.

//

\\

A good marriage
is honored by all.
It's deciding to
stay married for
better or worse.

//

\\

In marriage, you have to die to yourself daily.

//

\\

Building a good marriage meant you leave your past behind and committed to living the future with your spouse.

//

\\

If you love
something dearly,
you are willing to
wage war against
self-centeredness.

//

\\

True love is being committed to work out differences and leaving divorce as a non-viable option.

//

\\

Love is not
expecting what
to get but what
you can give.

//

\\

Finding a good
partner is like
having a steady
hand to lead you
through life.

//

\\

A good marriage
is having to
experience life
together
extraordinarily.

//

\\

Loving deeply is
having something
to hope for in
the future.

//

\\

The real marriage takes place in the self and not in a ceremony.

//

\\

Experiencing true love is like having the sun reflected on both sides.

//

\\

Being truly in
love is a ride
worth taking.

//

\\

In a committed
marriage,
you want the
happiness of the
other person
far more than
your own.

//

\\

Love sees
possibilities in
impossibilities.

//

\\

True love sees
beyond beauty.
It shares life with
another person
and staying in the
journey together.

//

\\

Love goes beyond
what the eye
can see.

//

\\

The highest experience you can get in this life is finding the right partner to take this journey with.

//

\\

Finding true love
is growing old with
someone you know
you can serve your
best years with.

//

\\

The start of
marriage is the
start of courtship.
It is the other
way around!

//

\\

Get married to the
one person you
can annoy with
your whole life.

//

\\

There's fulfillment
and joy in finding
the right person
to spend a
lifetime with!

//

\\

Marriage is the
fuel to the flame
of true love.

//

\\

Being married is finding a friend that gets caught up in a flame that turns into an unquenchable fire.

//

\\

To get the full
value of joy, you
need someone to
share it with.

//

\\

Successful marriages are those who found friendship in each others company.

//

\\

When you're in a
marriage, you
don't expect 50-50.
It's giving it your
best shot. That's
how you work
things together.

//

\\

No woman should marry a man if she hates his mother.

//

\\

Don't get married just to get married. Marry because you are mature and ready.

//

\\

Marriage is a cure to love's temporary insanity.

//

\\

A man has never
loved if he has
loved them all.

//

\\

True love is appreciating each other without taking possession.

//

\\

Marriage is like dancing to the tune of friendship set in the music.

//

\\

Deep love is a the fuel to a lasting marriage.

//

\\

Marriage is like
coffee that you
take everyday
and enjoyed.

//

\\

A marriage is flimsy if it's not rooted in deep convictions and commitment.

//

\\

Marriage is having
to consciously and
willingly forgive
each other.

//

\\

Marriage lets you see the other person as an imperfect being that you are willing to love perfectly.

//

\\

The tiny moments
you live with your
spouse are like
tiny blocks that
you build into
a castle.

//

\\

Mutual respect
is essential to
building lasting
marriages.

//

\\

People get into marriages because they want to stay locked in the relationship.

//

\\

Marriage doesn't change a person. It's simply celebrating them in a whole different light.

//

\\

The highest honor
you can give to
your spouse is
to love and
cherish them.

//

\\

True love comes from knowing that you believe in the same thing and are committed to finish the journey with a thankful heart.

//

\\

Coming together
is only the
beginning of
any marriage.

//

\\

You only progress
in your love for
each other once
you learn that you
cannot change
each other.

//

\\

Great marriages are created and not waited upon.

//

\\

There is nothing more comforting than for a man to find a good wife that will treasure and protect his love with her life.

//

\\

Marriage is the
habit of loving
each other daily.

//

\\

In life you marry three people: the one you think they are, the person they are the one you can spend your lifetime with.

//

\\

Marriage is
finding freedom to
be yourself
without inhibitions.

//

\\

You know you have found the right person when you know you anticipate sleepovers everyday with your best friend.

//

\\

In order to find the one, you have to be the one.

//

\\

If you have a good marriage, you become happier. If you have a bad one, you become a philosopher.

//

\\

You measure the
happiness of that
marriage by the
scars in their
tongues from
years of biting
angry remarks.

//

\\

A good marriage is having yourself wanting to come home everyday.

//

Other Titles By
The Grumpy Guru

Strong Women Quotes
Quotes About Changing
Success Quotes
Motivation Quotes
Dog Quotes
Boyfriend Quotes
Happiness Quotes
Quotes for Teachers
Inspiring Quotes
What A Life Quotes
Family Quotes
On Love Quotes
Best Friend Quotes
Quotes Friendship
Beach Quotes
Quotes for Life
Encouragement Quotes
Teamwork Quotes

Book Ordering

To order your copy / copies of
Marriage Quotes:
100 Lines, Sayings, Quotes for the Married

by The Grumpy Guru,
please visit: thegrumpy.guru.

You can also check out other titles
available.

Bulk Pricing and
Affiliate Programs Available

Printed in Great Britain
by Amazon